Saint Patrick

'A charming and elegant account'
Ireland of the Welcomes

'Dr Simms ... peels away the myth and
unearths a core that is even more fascinating
simply because it is true'
Sunday Press

'This book is filled with interesting little,
and superbly written, insights into the
real life of St Patrick'
Belfast Telegraph

'... Written in clear, lucid style'
Irish Echo

GEORGE OTTO SIMMS was born in Dublin in 1910. He took his BA, MA, BD, PhD and DD degrees at Trinity College, Dublin. Ordained a priest of the Church of Ireland in 1936, he spent his working life in the service of the Church and was Archbishop of Dublin from 1956 until 1969, and then Archbishop of Armagh and Primate of All Ireland from 1969 until his retirement in 1980. A respected scholar and historian, he lectured and wrote extensively, particularly on the Book of Kells, on which he was internationally recognised as an expert. For almost forty years he contributed a weekly religious feature, 'Thinking Aloud', to *The Irish Times*. *Exploring the Book of Kells* was Dr Simms's first book for the younger reader and it received wide acclaim. It won the Reading Association of Ireland Award, and together with his second book for children, *Brendan the Navigator, Exploring the Ancient World*, was joint winner of the Bisto Book of the Decade Award. George Otto Simms died in 1991.

SAINT PATRICK

IRELAND'S PATRON SAINT

GEORGE OTTO SIMMS

Drawings
DAVID ROONEY

THE O'BRIEN PRESS
DUBLIN

This revised edition first published 2004 by The O'Brien Press Ltd,
20 Victoria Road, Dublin 6, Ireland.
Tel: +353 1 4923333; Fax: +353 1 4922777
E-mail: books@obrien.ie
Website: www.obrien.ie
First published 1991. First published in paperback 1993.
Reprinted 1994, 1999.

ISBN 0-86278-749-1

British Library Cataloguing-in-Publication Data
A catalogue record for this book is available from the British Library.

5 6 7 8 9 10
04 05 06 07 08 09

Editing, layout, design and typesetting: The O'Brien Press Ltd
Drawings: David Rooney
Drawings from the Book of Armagh: Eoin O'Brien
Printing: Betaprint Ltd

PICTURE CREDITS AND ACKNOWLEDGEMENTS

The publisher wishes to thank the following for permission to reproduce images.
Front cover: Broighter ship, sword hilt and Shrine of St Patrick's Bell courtesy of the
National Museum of Ireland; statue of Saint Patrick courtesy of George Munday and
The Irish Image Collection (www.theirishimagecollection.ie). **Back cover:** carving of St
Patrick, Faughart graveyard, Co. Louth, courtesy of the National Museum of Ireland.
Colour section: courtesy of George Munday and The Irish Image Collection: p.2 (top),
p.3 (top and bottom), p.4 (top and bottom), p. 5 (top and bottom), p.8; courtesy of
Michael Fox and www.knowth.com: p.1 (bottom); courtesy of the Archives Office, St
Patrick's Cathedral, Dublin, and www.stpatrickscathedral.ie: p.1 (top), p.2 (bottom); cour-
tesy of St Patrick's Festival, Dublin (www.stpatricksfestival.ie): p.6 (top); courtesy of James
Casserly and www.stpatricksday.com, p.6 (bottom); courtesy of Martin Schmitz and
www.ganz-muenchen.de: p.7 (top); courtesy of Tom Felle and the *Irish Echo*: p.7 (bottom).

Contents

FOREWORD

St Patrick's Cathedral probably owes its dedication to a well at the northwest corner of the grounds, which had an early association with the saint. Nowadays, St Patrick has become a household name – both here and abroad – and he enjoys a level of devotion, particularly in Ireland, that is almost unique. His popularity is enhanced by the fact that we have two pieces of authentic writing by him in the *Confession* and the *Letter to Coroticus*, which, as George Otto Simms shows, allows him to come to life for us in a very real way, as both man and saint.

But what we have been slow to learn from Patrick and the Church he founded in Ireland is that there is more than one model of Church available to us. Both the Church of Ireland and the Roman Catholic Church are, in their organisation, products of the feudal system which held sway all over medieval Europe and was based on a hierarchical structure. The Church that Patrick founded, however, was different: it was modelled as a community. There were bishops, certainly, but they were bishops *in community*. It was a harmonious and peaceful religious society – a reflection of Patrick's ideals of tolerance and togetherness.

George Otto Simms has written widely about Patrick's Celtic world, and many will also remember his famous lectures on the Book of Kells. He was without doubt the most influential figure in the Church of Ireland during the latter half of the twentieth century. He served as Archbishop of Dublin from 1956 until 1969, and under his leadership the Church of Ireland came out of the ghetto and into modern Ireland. Archbishop Simms was both an Irish speaker and an Irish scholar, and his right to make a contribution to Irish Christianity could not be seriously questioned. The willingness of the Church of Ireland to open its Christian assemblies to Roman Catholic participation – a move pioneered by Archbishop Simms – met with a warm welcome. As a result of his guidance and perseverance, a new atmosphere began to pervade Irish public life – indeed, very soon the situation became that with which we are now well accustomed: that no 'happening' in any local community is complete without the presence and participation of the local rector, alongside the parish priest. George Otto Simms made ecumenism possible.

Here at St Patrick's Cathedral, we remember fondly a man, an archbishop and an author who occupied the pulpit frequently, who spoke with compassion and intelligence and who was always careful to observe his weeks of residence as Prebendary of Cualaun. Archbishop George Otto Simms left an important and enduring legacy for the Irish people, and we are grateful to him for that.

Robert MacCarthy
Dean of St Patrick's Cathedral, Dublin

PART I

Patrick begins to write his Letter *and his* Confession
in humble words: 'Ego Patricius' –
'I, Patrick, a sinner'.

CHAPTER 1

What Patrick Wrote

Saint Patrick has left us a *Letter* which he wrote, in Latin, fifteen hundred years ago. Later on in his life he also wrote, or dictated to a secretary, a personal account of his work as a bishop in Ireland. This piece of writing, called by some his *Confession*, tells all who read it much about Patrick as a man and as a Christian who loved to serve God by caring for people. Writing in his old age, he looks back on his life, which he admits was full of faults and shortcomings. In the end, however, he is deeply thankful for what he was called to do among the people of Ireland. The *Confession* is not a simple biography, nor does it concentrate solely on his failures; it is much more a thanksgiving and a meditation full of praise for the goodness God showed to him in all the dangers and hazards of a life full of adventure and activity.

The *Confession* and the *Letter* to the soldiers under the

command of their chieftain, Coroticus, are recognised widely as containing Patrick's own thoughts and words. Patrick himself has, as it were, given us a picture of his personality. As we read the *Confession* and the *Letter* we try to capture his appearance, the expression on his face, his character, his firm faith, his humble approach to the great task that was assigned to him. There is much more to be discovered about him: he is more than a name, more than a legend, more than a symbol of Ireland and the Irish wherever they live. He is a saint and, as has been said, 'saints are not made by accident'. They are part of history. Indeed, someone said that saints were those who did ordinary things extraordinarily well.

The aim of this character sketch is to distinguish between what actually happened in Patrick's life and the many later stories, often legendary but also embodying truths about him, which have circulated in his honour. There are memoirs, biographies, hymns and unwritten traditions associating him with people and places throughout the length and breadth of Ireland. These are signs of his popularity. Such traditions reveal the inspiration of a leader and a teacher who spread the good news of Christianity on his travels, through many an encounter with strangers and friends. He had enemies too. His spiritual victories were never claimed by him as personal achievements. He gave the glory and the honour to the God whom he came to know intimately when he arrived in Ireland as a slave boy. He lived to call himself God's slave and servant. In God's service he learnt the secret of a true and perfect freedom.

CHAPTER 2

Ireland in the Days before Patrick

Seafarers and adventurers sailing out from the Mediterranean looked upon Ireland as the last piece of land on their journey out west.

Those who landed upon the Irish coast were reluctant to penetrate the uncharted waters of the mysterious Atlantic Ocean. Explorations came to a full stop at this outer edge of the continent of Europe. The island of Ireland was known sometimes as 'the back of beyond', or in Latin as *ultima Thule*, the last stop on the voyage.

Greek writers knew about Ireland. Strabo the geographer called it *Ierne*. Latin writers named the island *Hibernia* when they wrote about the Celts of Gaul (France) and the Druids.

The Celts came westward from mid-Europe to Britain,

reaching Ireland about three hundred years before Christ. In Britain, they had organised themselves well enough to resist Julius Caesar and his military forces in the campaign of 55BC.

Celtic culture had already taken root as a distinctive part of Ireland's ancient heritage when Patrick first arrived as a boy in his 'teens, as a slave captured to serve an unknown master.

The Ireland of Patrick's day, in the fifth century AD, had a very small population – a mere quarter-of-a-million inhabitants, compared with today's four-and-a-half million. Their livelihood depended on the rearing of cattle and sheep and also mixed farming. Thick forests covered large tracts of land. The word for 'road' was, understandably, *bóthar*, meaning a path for the cows.

About one hundred chieftains ruled as petty kings among their clans, up and down the country. Remarkably enough, we learn that, within a hundred years of Patrick's death, these warrior-kings had become Christian. Their form of government, their organisation as families and local communities, continued as before. Their judges, or brehons, administered the laws and kept the peace. The druids continued to advise their rulers. In Ireland during the early days of the Christian Church no martyr's blood seems to have been shed. The physical persecution that caused so much suffering in other countries did not accompany the introduction of the Christian Gospel to Ireland.

There were no cities at that time. Later, from the sixth century, monasteries were the centres of life and activity.

*An Early Celtic settlement – the ring-fort enclosing the
dwellings was typical of the normal homesteads of the farming
communities in Early Celtic Ireland.*

They provided places of education and learning as well as
churches for worship and spiritual life. Through their
scribes and scholars, the art of writing was introduced to
Ireland. The earlier *ogham* script consisted of lines and
dots. The psalm books and Christian Gospels were copied
and circulated in Latin, the language which many of the
European countries had in common. Those who came to
Ireland, and later the missionaries who went out from
Ireland to the Continent, shared this *lingua franca*, this
common language of worship, study and teaching. Latin
was the language of the educated European.

Before this, Irish was the spoken language. The history
and traditions of the country were oral. Many stories and
wise sayings well remembered were passed on from
mouth to mouth.

An ogham *(or* ogam*)*
stone from the
Early Christian period.

Storytelling was an important means of communication. Not surprisingly, many legends circulated around people and places. Important events, such as battles, storms, cattle-raids, plagues and famines, were remembered. The description of them often became highly coloured when told by dramatic storytellers who passed on picturesque and evermore vivid accounts of great moments of victory or disaster in the past.

The Venerable Bede, who was born more than two hundred years after St Patrick, writes about Ireland in his famous book, *A History of the English Church and People*. Living in Jarrow, in Northumbria, he admires the faith and learning of the monasteries in Ireland. He used to recommend his students to spend time there in the course of their training. He wrote that 'Ireland is far more favoured than Britain by latitude, and by its mild and healthy climate. Snow rarely lies longer than three days, so that there is no need to store hay in summer for winter use, or to build stables for beasts. There are no reptiles, and no snake can exist there; for although often brought over from Britain, as soon as the ship nears land, they breathe the scent of its air and die.'

Bede mentions Irish pirates attacking the coastline of Britain. Strangely enough, he has apparently nothing to tell us about Patrick. He mentions Columba frequently, but makes us wonder why, after his account of Palladius – who was sent by Pope Celestine 'to the Scots [the Irish] who believed in Christ to be their first bishop' – there was no reference to Patrick who came so soon afterwards. We can be sure, however, that, even if nothing survived in writing for such a long time, Patrick was very much in the conversation and storytelling throughout the whole countryside.

CHAPTER 3

History Comes to Light

There is always great excitement in a household when someone in the family drags out from a dark corner under the stairs a forgotten tin-box full of letters written by grandparents or great-aunts in times past. Perhaps the box has not been opened during the lifetime of the youngest members of the family. Suddenly they discover that their relations from generations long ago are real people, not merely dim and distant names.

As they read the letters, the writers quickly become personalities. A little bit of family history comes to life. Cries of surprise and peals of laughter are heard when the old-fashioned style of writing is read aloud around the fireside. Names of places in the neighbourhood, well-known today, are mentioned in these dusty letters, already turning yellow with age.

The Lion – the symbol of St Mark's Gospel –
from the Book of Armagh.

Sometimes old diaries also turn up to give us news of happenings completely unheard of, or forgotten. Account books and receipts tell a story of the cost of living in the old days. Everyone's curiosity is aroused. Questions are asked when the meaning is not clear. Genuine history comes out of this inquiry into the past. The family realises that its members, from the oldest to the youngest, are making history every day. The old letters and all the details in the diaries remind the family of its traditions and heritage.

Some of this kind of excitement was felt in Ireland when all the learned scholars and students of Patrick's life and work agreed that a personal letter, allegedly from Patrick, and a kind of diary, called his *Confession*, really were written by the saint himself about fifteen hundred years ago.

These two pieces of writing are very precious. In days long before printing was invented, they were copied many times by writers of manuscripts into books written by hand. It is thought that Irish history, as recorded in writing, began with Patrick's *Letter* to the soldiers of Coroticus and his *Confession*. They were written in the fifth century AD. The oldest copies, however, date from about one thousand years ago. These are kept in libraries, as special treasures; some in Brussels, Paris, London and Oxford and others in different towns in Europe. Part of the *Confession*, the writing that Patrick handed on in his old age to his Christian friends, is kept in the Library of Trinity College, Dublin, within the covers of the ninth-century Book of Armagh, written by hand, with some fascinating pen-drawings.

Today it is generally accepted that the *Confession* and the *Letter* are from the pen of Patrick.

We are going to explore these documents. We will find that Patrick is more than the mere name of a famous saint, well-known throughout the world, but especially admired in Ireland. We will discover many things about him. We learn about his early days as a boy at home with his parents. When we read what he wrote about himself we learn that he was kidnapped and carried off as a slave. He tells us what his Christian faith meant to him in lonely days of great suffering. His many adventures show us how brave and strong he was in very hard times. These writings introduce us to a very important person, an outstanding hero, about whom many stories were told in later days.

A handwritten page from the Book of Armagh. The opening of Patrick's Confession, 'Ego Patricius', is in the left-hand column, nine lines down from the top.

We are going to find out what he was really like, by reading his own words. The manner in which he tells us about himself, without any boasting, makes us realise that we are in touch with the flesh-and-blood Patrick. As the saying goes, he describes himself 'warts and all'. He is not afraid to point out his weaknesses, but he stands up for the faith in which he had put his trust and firmly defends the God who has guided and protected him, in the teeth of hostile criticism.

When Patrick writes, he begins with such honest words as, 'I, Patrick, a sinner', and immediately we warm to him.

CHAPTER 4

Patrick's Youth

Patrick lived in Britain as a boy, where he grew up in a place called Bannavem Taberniae. We think Bannavem was not far from the sea, on the west coast, perhaps in what is now known as Cumbria. His birthplace was probably a village rather than a large town. It has not been possible to find the exact spot on the map. Others think that Bannavem might have been near the coast of Wales. However, Patterdale, in the Lake District, recalls in its name a well of Patrick; perhaps this was where he was born. We do not know. We have to make many guesses about places and dates when little has been written down about them.

We guess that he lived not far from the sea because he was snatched away from home by a ship's crew from Ireland. Quite often ships would cross the Irish sea to trade with Britain. Sometimes pirates rather than merchant sailors would raid the coast in search of plunder. The narrow strip of water between Ireland and the region near Carlisle and the famous wall erected by the Roman Emperor Hadrian made these invasions a common occurrence.

Before Patrick was born, Britain had been an outpost of the great Roman Empire. Rome, the capital city, was attacked and destroyed in the year AD410. The Empire was no longer so great. Its 'decline and fall' began after invading armies of Goths swept across from the southeast of Europe to win victories over Rome's imperial armies.

In Britain, however, life went on despite these shattering disasters. All was changed. Britain and Gaul (France) had been governed together as one province by the Roman powers. Now, instead of being ruled by an emperor and others authorised by him from the distant capital city, the citizens in Patrick's home district were governed by officials appointed locally. Patrick's father was one of these officials.

LIFE AT HOME

Patrick's parents lived in a villa. There was a farm attached to the home. His father, Calpurnius, belonged to a group of leading citizens who made sure that the laws were kept and the taxes were paid. Order had to be kept on the roads and in the market place. The official name for each of these keepers of the peace was *decurio,* a Latin title used in the Empire.

THE LAST DAYS OF THE EMPIRE

Britain was very fortunate to have good roads throughout the country. There were many thoroughfares, running in straight lines, expertly planned by engineers and soldiers. They linked city with city, and one fortified camp with another. There are still great stretches of road without a bend or a turn in England today. The Great North Road and the famous Watling Street remind travellers of Britain's early history.

The City of London owes much to the builders and developers of the great days of the Roman Empire. For some four hundred years, fine buildings were constructed in many parts of the country. Theatres, baths, handsome archways and stately villas were built in the beautifully designed towns. Recent excavations have shown how skilful artists as well as expert architects were at work in centres such as York, in the north, and St Albans, near London. Mosaic floors of great beauty and finely sculpted statues survive to recall the grandeur of those days. After the severe bombing of the City of London during the Second World War (1939–1945), many traces of the Roman occupation of the first centuries of the Christian era were found. When the rubble of the shattered buildings was removed, fragments of pillared temples and decorated houses were uncovered.

HE LEFT SCHOOL TOO EARLY

Patrick was probably educated at home by his parents and perhaps also by one of the servants who worked on the

*The remains of a Romano-British mosaic floor at Hinton
St Mary in Somerset. This shows Christ and the Evangelists and
probably dates from AD335–55.*

estate. He seems to have been very much attached to the
life on the farm in those early days. He mentions men-
servants and women-servants, all of whom he counted as
part of the larger family, belonging to the household at the
villa. The servants were, in fact, slaves. They had little personal freedom. As citizens, they had no share in the decisions that had to be made in the public affairs of the village.
They were not given a vote. However, we do know that
slaves were often treated very well by their masters. We
get the impression that Patrick's home was a happy one.

The villa may not have been as large or luxurious as some other homes, but it was comfortable and there seems to have been a friendly feeling among all in the house.

It was a Christian home. Calpurnius was not only a civil servant (*decurio*), he also had an official position in the life of the Church as a deacon. He undertook duties during the Church's services of worship. He would also visit the faithful when they were sick or in any kind of need. He was in a position to give them help and advice when they had problems and worries.

Patrick's grandfather, Potitus, was a priest (*presbyter* in Latin). Evidently there had been organised Church life in that part of Britain for more than one generation. In later days, Patrick hinted that his Christian faith meant much more to him when he was on his own, away from home and feeling the pain of loneliness.

A NAME TO REMEMBER

No one is quite sure of the meaning of the name Bannavem Taberniae, but some guesses have been made. *Banna* might refer to a rock, rising up steeply from the plain. *Vem* may be a Celtic word for a market place. The *bern* in Ta*bern*iae could stand for a gap (*bearna* in Irish) in the hills. There are several places along Hadrian's Wall, which divides present-day England from Scotland, where standing rocks at the head of a valley act as landmarks at which people used to gather.

The name of his hometown indicates that this was Celtic-British country, where a local Celtic language would be used by the people in ordinary conversation.

Patrick's lessons as a schoolboy would have been given in Latin, the language of the Empire. The Romans had brought their language with them as well as their roads, their buildings, their laws, their system of coinage and their skilled engineers and builders.

Patrick wrote very modestly and humbly about his knowledge of Latin. He had a strong feeling during his life that he had not been nearly as well educated as many of his friends and neighbours. He mentions several times in his *Confession* that he had only a very rough-and-ready way of putting down in writing what he wanted to say. He felt that this was a real handicap. There is the feeling, nevertheless, when we read what he wrote, that in fact Patrick was certainly most intelligent. He would have progressed very well with his lessons had he not been cruelly prevented from continuing his education at a very important moment in his career. An interruption occurred which was to change his whole life.

CHAPTER 5

He is Captured and Carried Off to Ireland

Patrick was taken captive. He was snatched away from his comfortable home just before his sixteenth birthday. It all happened very suddenly. A ship came over from Ireland in search of plunder and slave labour. Slaves were valuable. They could be sold for gold and precious stones, or used as labourers on the land with farmers as their masters. Patrick was not the only one to be seized and taken on board that fateful day. A whole gang of captives was bundled into the ship. They were tied up and carried off to Ireland by force. Patrick wrote that he was one among thousands kidnapped that day.

'I, Patrick, a sinner, was captured when about sixteen years old. I did
not then know the true God. Like thousands of others, I was carried
into captivity – and we deserved it.'

TO BE A SLAVE

Next we hear of him far away in the west of Ireland. He was engaged by his new master to work on a farm that seems to have been near 'the woods of Foclut, by the western sea' in Co. Mayo. This is the only place in Ireland that Patrick mentions. He says nothing about Tara, Slemish, Downpatrick, or Armagh – the places often associated with him. He had to look after the sheep. He was responsible for protecting the flock from savage attacks by wild animals. If some sheep wandered away and were lost in the woods or on the mountain, Patrick would have to search for them. It was a hard life working outdoors in all kinds of weather.

TO FIND A FAITH

Patrick felt the loneliness of it all. Yet, the long hours spent on his own gave him many opportunities to think about life and the future. He has written that he began to think about God in quite a new way. Through his thoughts and his prayers he came to know God as a friend and companion. He said as many as a hundred prayers every day.

PRAYER WAS HIS LIFE

Through these prayers he kept a conversation going with God while on his own under the open sky. He admitted that when he was a boy at home God had seemed very far away. 'I did not then know the true God,' he tells us. Now things were different. Even on sharp frosty nights when he sheltered in his little shepherd's hut, he would feel the warmth of the Holy Spirit's power in his veins and through his whole body. Many years after his death, the prayers he used were woven into a song called 'St Patrick's Breastplate' (the *'Lorica'*). These words echoed Patrick's feelings and experiences. They have a lovely rhythm and are often sung today.

Christ be within me,
Christ be beside me,
Christ be behind me,
Christ be before me.

They catch the spirit of his newly found faith.

PATRICK – A NEW MAN

He found the creed, which he had learned by heart as a boy, coming to life in a remarkable way. His experiences were teaching him fresh things about God's love and protection. He was not afraid anymore. His trust in God and his love for Him drove away his old fears.

BRAVELY HUMBLE

Patrick found it very difficult to put these spiritual experiences into words. He felt that if he had been fully educated he could have explained to others something of the joy and the confidence he had in believing God and in trusting Him. He took courage from the description of Isaiah's feelings when that great prophet wrote: 'The tongue of the stammerers shall be ready to speak plainly.'

Patrick certainly knew the scriptures. He was also able to express himself in writing and hardly deserves to be called 'ignorant'. He thought of himself as a country fellow and used country expressions so that he might be better understood by his readers.

VISIONS AND DREAMS

Patrick's prayers came from the heart. They helped him to keep up his courage in the work he had to do. Soon a vision of his future came to him while he slept. He believed that he really deserved the life of a slave in captivity because in his youth his life had been full of faults and failures. Now he was beginning to see how much the hard life was teaching him. He knew in his heart that God was showing him the right way.

In one particular vision, he saw himself as a lifeless, useless stone, stuck in the mud and unable to move. Then something happened. Patrick described his dream: 'He that is mighty,' he wrote, 'took hold of me, lifted me out of the mud, and set me up on top of the wall.' The stone that was Patrick had fallen off the wall and was now put back in an important place. Was there stony country all around him, as in the west of Ireland today? It looked as if, with God's help and not through any special cleverness on Patrick's part, he was being chosen for some responsible work in the future. He was marked out to be a leader.

More visions and dreams were to follow. He wrote about these vivid and lively thoughts which chased

'I was like a stone lying in deep mud and He that
is mighty lifted me up.'

through his mind while he slept. These visions were like pictures. The longer he looked at them, the more details he saw. A dream is often very puzzling and fleeting at first. Gradually its meaning becomes clearer. Patrick began to feel very sure that he was being shown the way forward, step by step, into the unknown future that lay before him.

CHAPTER 6

Escape to Freedom

Once, when Patrick was out in the woods, on the mountain slopes, he heard a voice in the night. He had been praying, as usual.

'Your ship is ready,' the voice announced.

This was very strange. What ship? Patrick wondered. He was nowhere near any of the harbours, which were far away on the east coast of Ireland. He knew that merchant ships frequently crossed the sea to Britain or Gaul, but in Co. Mayo he seemed to be on the edge of the world, at the very farthest point of Europe. No ships would sail westwards into the mysterious, unexplored ocean of the Atlantic. That would be impossible. He could not have been called to go 'over the edge' into the blue and the great unknown, away from people.

So the voice must have been urging him to travel eastwards. Although he knew no one and felt a complete

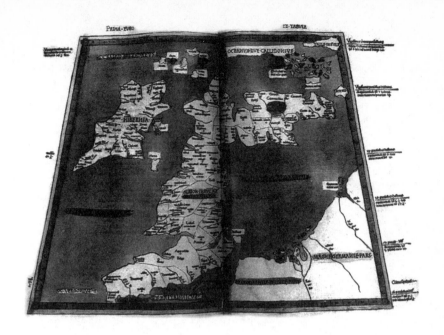

Ptolemy's map, the earliest known map of Ireland,
drawn in the second century AD.

stranger, he started on the two-hundred-mile journey to the east coast. Great courage was needed for this adventure. He was leaving the master whom he had been serving for the past six years. He hints that he was in some ways sorry to be going away, in spite of the hard times he had faced. Did he think that he was letting his master down? Who would look after the sheep that he had cared for? Was he right to turn his back on the life to which he had become accustomed and go off to some unknown and distant spot? It was like plunging into a deep and dark hole.

Apparently, he had never tried to escape from his master and become a runaway. His master, even if strict, may have been kindly and humane. His good qualities may have struck Patrick after he had left service. The dream, however, convinced him that he must go. Those words about the ship had sounded loud and clear. He never forgot them, even in his old age. Nor did fear hold him back. He never felt afraid because he had an inner confidence that God would lead him. A new life was opening up before him. He was in a cheerful mood and full of expectation when he came at last to the seashore and there, before his eyes, was the ship of his vision.

TAKEN ON BOARD

The ship was on the point of moving out to sea when Patrick arrived. It had already been untied from its moorings. The anchor was raised. Patrick was only just in time to have a word with the crew. He asked about the voyage they were undertaking and politely sounded them out about the possibility of joining them on board. Whatever the ordinary members of the ship's crew thought about the suggestion that Patrick should be given a lift across the water, it was quite clear that the captain was strongly against the idea. He brushed Patrick off with an angry refusal. He used a Latin word, *nequaquam*, which might be translated by the modern phrase, 'No way'. The captain was extremely emphatic and bluntly rude. 'No way, no way will you be coming with us!' he shouted.

He sounded rather like those bullies who appear so sure of themselves, when, in fact, they are covering up their own fears. But this loud-voiced captain, for all his blustering, may have sensed in Patrick's manner and gentle approach something that made him wonder about this young traveller. Patrick seems to have been someone out of the ordinary. The captain began to have doubts. To refuse to take Patrick on board might bring bad luck.

So the conversation did not end there. Patrick walked away from the ship and back to the little hut on the shore where he had spent the previous night. There he began to pray, turning to God as to a faithful friend. Meanwhile, the captain was having second thoughts. After all, Patrick did not look like an ordinary stowaway. His pleasant manner, which was to charm many people throughout his active life, certainly did not suggest that he was an undesirable person escaping from some kind of trouble. Nor did he look as if he were flying away from the clutches of a pursuer.

To Patrick's surprise, a shout came from the direction of the boat.

'Come back, quickly!' they were shouting. 'Come, we will take you with us. We trust you. Make friends with us!'

Clearly they had begun to think differently about this stranger. He appeared to have good intentions in his heart. They were no longer suspicious of him. Indeed they might be very glad to have him with them on board; he might bring them good luck.

They themselves were not Christians, but they were beginning to see that the journey might be more successful with Patrick than without him. While Patrick saw in their invitation an answer to his prayer: the captain had changed his mind.

Off they sailed together. They were three whole days at sea before they reached land on the opposite shore. From

'The ship's captain said angrily:
"No way are you going to come aboard with us."'

Patrick's account of the voyage, it is not clear whether the harbour that they reached was in Britain, or on the French coast. Most people think that they landed in Britain, perhaps somewhere on the coast of Wales, or even further south, off Cornwall.

LOST AND FOUND

When the ship reached land, the crew and Patrick set off across the country. By this time, all in the ship had come to admire him. They were very happy that he should stay with them. They lost their way more than once. They could very easily have gone around in circles as there would have been very few paths or woodland tracks to guide them, and no familiar landmarks to show them where they were going. We can picture the misery and despair that they must have felt, when they seemed to be making no progress.

They were a full twenty-eight days on the move across country before they found anything to eat.

'We ran out of food,' Patrick wrote, recalling this uncomfortable experience. 'The captain of the ship came up to me and said, "You who are a Christian, can you explain the meaning of all this? You say that your God is great and all-powerful. Why are you not able to pray to Him for us? Here we are, perishing with hunger and we can scarcely believe that we will ever again see another human being."'

Patrick replied, speaking with great assurance. 'Turn with complete trust to my Lord and God. Turn to Him with all your heart. Ask Him today for food, so that He may arrange for you all to have enough to satisfy your appetites.

You will certainly be fed, because He has a plentiful supply of food everywhere.'

Everything turned out well after that. A herd of pigs suddenly appeared on the path before them. They killed a great number of them. Then they stayed for two nights in that spot and ate their fill. Their bodies, which had grown weak and tired from hunger, were restored to their former strength. They all gave thanks enthusiastically to the God who had rescued them. Patrick became a hero. His shipmates paid him great respect. On the following days, they had plenty of food. They found some wild honey and offered a little to Patrick, asking him to taste it and saying, 'This is a sacrifice.' These words suggested pagan worship. Patrick, somewhat embarrassed, did not accept this kind of offering. He was reluctant to join in a ceremony that was clearly not Christian. He thanked God, whom he had come to regard as a friend, that he had been guided not to share in this kind of superstitious ceremony, which implied that God was to be feared rather than loved.

HOME AGAIN

After these wanderings were over, Patrick returned home to his parents. They were overjoyed to welcome him back and hoped that he would never again be taken from them. Little did they know, however, what had happened to their son. His time in Ireland had completely changed his outlook on life. Now he saw everything at home in a very different light.

MORE VISIONS AND VOICES

One night the prophet Elijah came to Patrick in a dream. In the Old Testament, Elijah had influenced the kings of his day. In some ways this particular prophet was a lonely figure who had to say unpopular things to people in power when the country was in danger. He was the prophet who heard a voice bringing him a message from God. It was a still, small voice. God did not speak to him in a thunderstorm, or a rushing wind, or in the flames of a fire, but rather in a quiet way, without any showy, sensational signs.

Patrick felt that he also had a bright future in front of him. If he was not to be a prophet, he would certainly be a servant of God. A 'still, small voice' was calling him too.

Dreams are often confusing. In Patrick's mind the Hebrew name *Elijah* was mixed up with the Greek word *Hélios*, meaning the sun. The dream threw light upon his dark future. Christ had often been called 'the true light' and was even given the title of 'the sun of righteousness'. All these ideas came into the dream.

Fortunately this dream, which had started in rather a terrifying way with a great rock falling on Patrick's body and pinning him to the ground, ended happily. He thought no more of Elijah's misery and unpopularity, for the sun shone through and changed the whole scene of dark suffering into a brilliant, bright view of the countryside. A voice gave him courage. It assured him that when he preached about Christ to others, it was not he, Patrick, who was speaking the words. It was the spirit of God speaking in him.

'One night, in my dreams, I saw a man delivering letters with the invitation, "Come and walk among us again".'

IRELAND CALLING

Patrick's next vision was crucial. It was quite startling. This time the voice was 'the cry of the Irish'. In his dream he saw a man called Victoricus standing in front of him. In his hand he held a whole sheaf of letters, which seemed to be written messages and notes from all sorts of people in Ireland. They were asking Patrick to come over to Ireland and be with them again. He seemed to see them crowding around the trees in the forest of Foclut 'by the western sea', which looked just like the Mayo country he had known so well.

The voice went on: 'Holy boy, we ask you to come and walk among us once again.'

The invitation was most pressing. Patrick felt like the apostle Paul who had had a dream many years earlier in which a manly voice from Macedonia cried out: 'Come over, and help us.' As a result, Paul, who was at Troy in Asia, crossed over to Europe by boat with the good news of the Christian Gospel. So the message of Christ passed from one continent to another.

Victoricus stands out in the story of Patrick as a very important figure. He is the only person in Ireland mentioned in Patrick's *Confession*.

DREAMS COME TRUE

Dreams of this sort continued. They gave Patrick great encouragement as he prepared himself for the work that lay ahead. Sometimes these dreams were warnings. They showed him what a difficult task he was undertaking. One

45

night he was greatly delighted when he heard the familiar, unmistakable voice tell him confidentially, 'He who gave His life for you, He it is who speaks in you.' Patrick woke up, overjoyed. This was surely a genuine call. He must obey it.

Soon he learned new things about God and prayer. He was careful not to think that he knew all the answers to the questions that faced him. He realised that as a result of the hard and painful times he had endured, he had learned to be humble and never to be self-satisfied.

PATRICK DEFENDS HIMSELF

Patrick was a very sensitive person. He felt things deeply. This was part of his greatness. He was concerned about other people and kept thinking of ways in which he could help them. He shared their difficulties and troubles.

Patrick became very worried when he heard that some of the older members of the Church, his seniors, disapproved of the suggestion that he should be sent to Ireland as a bishop.

Some of these seniors wanted him to remain in Britain. Others had heard that his behaviour in his youth had not been free from faults. They doubted if he was really fit to undertake the sacred duties of the Church's ministry, in spite of the training he had received in the years after his captivity in Ireland. There were unpleasant rumours circulating about his misspent youth. Had he turned to pagan worship and superstition? We simply do not know what faults they were referring to.

Patrick admitted that as a fifteen-year-old he had felt guilty about himself and his life. He was quite depressed about it. He told a close friend about this worry and, at the time, this sharing of his burden with another appeared to bring great relief. The friend did not cease to be a friend after hearing all that Patrick had to say. Indeed, the friend, who was a great admirer of Patrick, had gone so far as to tell him, 'You should be raised to the rank of a bishop.'

Imagine, then, the shock which followed when this close friend to whom Patrick had 'entrusted his soul', broke confidence and told the Church authorities about this dark secret of long ago. Patrick was greatly taken aback.

In sorrow rather than in anger, and certainly without any bitterness, he said: 'How did my close friend take it into his head, afterwards, publicly, before everyone – both those who wished me well and my enemies who were ill-disposed to me – to discredit me for something which he had, of his own accord, been glad to pardon me? The Lord, also, who is greater than all, had granted me pardon.'

GOD IS ON HIS SIDE

The last vision that Patrick wrote about gave him fresh hope after all the agonies he had suffered, and restored his confidence in himself. During the night he saw some writing. He found it hard to describe the details of this vision, but he seems to have seen his own face on a coin. The heads of Roman emperors were often engraved on coins with words of praise and honour inscribed in letters encircling the head. In his dream, Patrick read not words of honour but words of shame and disgrace surrounding his head. This seemed to be a sign that he was rejected and dishonoured. In fact, this was not so. Together with the vision, he heard a voice from God which said: 'We have seen with displeasure the face of the man denounced here.'

Patrick took note that the words were not *you* have seen' but *we* have seen'. He knew that God was on his side. God was supporting Patrick, not denouncing him. God disapproved of the words which attempted to damage Patrick's reputation and blacken his character.

These visions tell us more than mere words can express about those searching days of preparation before Patrick eventually set out to bring the Christian faith to Ireland.

Above: An image of Saint Patrick from the altar frontal in Saint Patrick's Cathedral, Dublin.

Left: Patrick's life took many strange twists and turns in his journey from slave to saint. This is the Mound of the Hostages on the Hill of Tara, Co. Meath, where, it is said, Patrick was held captive before being sold to a new master in the west of Ireland.

Above: Worldwide, Saint Patrick is synonymous with the snakes he is said to have banished from Ireland – this is the most enduring myth about the saint.

Below: The beautiful stained-glass windows in Saint Patrick's Cathedral, Dublin, record the life of Patrick, man and saint.

Opposite page

Top: The interior of Saint Patrick's Cathedral, Dublin.

Bottom: It is said that Saint Patrick's body lies in Downpatrick graveyard, on the grounds of the cathedral, and that his final resting place is marked by a flat boulder stone.

Left: Statue of Saint Patrick on Downpatrick Head in Co. Mayo, a place of pilgrimage for followers of the saint.

Below: In Ireland, there are many wells (*tobar*) and 'beds', or gravestones (*leaba*) dedicated to various saints. Near Ballyshannon in Donegal, a small cross marks the spot of the Holy Well of Saint Patrick, a place held sacred to the saint's name. The tree is laden with coloured rags, each one representing a petition to the saint.

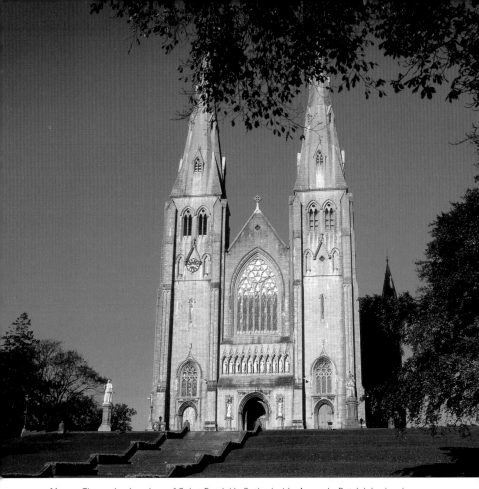

Above: The majestic spires of Saint Patrick's Cathedral in Armagh. Patrick is closely associated with Armagh, which, the Book of the Angel tells us, he 'loved more than all the lands of the Irish'.

Below: A panoramic view of Clew Bay with the pointed peak of Croagh Patrick rising in the distance. This is a place of annual pilgrimage for thousands of people who climb the mountain – many barefoot – in order to pay homage to Saint Patrick and to pray in the tiny church on the summit.

Above: Saint Patrick's feast day, 17 March – the date recorded in the Book of Armagh as the date of his death – has become a day of celebration across the world. In Dublin, the festival has become a week-long event and thousands of visitors throng the streets, adding to the carnival atmosphere generated by the festival performers.

Below: The parade in New York dates back to 1762. It has become a huge annual event, with participants from many different countries. These Irish dancers are making their way down Fifth Avenue to the strains of the accordion.

Above: Crowds line the streets of Munich, in Germany, to celebrate Saint Patrick's Day.
Below: Australia has a large population that claims Irish descent, and Saint Patrick's Day is an important day for coming together. These children in Sydney are enjoying that rare thing: a sun-drenched Saint Patrick's Day!

Above: This statue of the saint stands on the Hill of Tara in Co. Meath. Now a household name the world over, Saint Patrick conjures up many different images: from snakes to croziers and from parades to cathedrals. But his lasting legacy is his lesson of benevolence, tolerance and Christian living, and his promise to watch over the people of Ireland.

CHAPTER 7

In Ireland Again

Patrick had been instructed in the teaching of the Church while near his home in Britain. He probably received further training in a monastery in Gaul as he prepared for ordination. The name of Germanus, Bishop of Auxerre in France, was well-known as a leader in both Britain and Gaul. Many think that Patrick came under his influence during his years of training. After this he was commissioned as a bishop to serve in Ireland.

His calling had been heard clearly. He had not taken vows as a monk, but he was familiar with the life of prayer, study and practical work that was typical among those who lived in a monastic community. Patrick was steeped in the scriptures and there were many quotations from the Bible in his writings. He was a man of constant prayer. His love for people was quite remarkable. We have only a few details about the years that led up to his missionary journey back to the island to which he had originally been taken by force. He had suffered much but, looking back on it all, he realised that he had gained far more than he had lost during those years of slavery.

CHRISTIANS IN IRELAND BEFORE PATRICK

There were Christians in Ireland before Patrick's mission began. Prosper of Aquitaine, in his *Chronicle*, records: 'Palladius was ordained and sent as first bishop to the Irish who believed in Christ by Pope Celestine,' in the year AD431. We do not know very much more about Palladius and the journey he took to this outpost of Europe. His name appears in one of the early Church calendars.

Tradition claims that other Christians, such as Declan from the Waterford area, were in Ireland before Patrick. Shipping and trading from France and Wales provided a link and a contact. Visitors and travellers from the continent to Ireland would in all likelihood have had Christians among their company.

PATRICK'S BELIEFS

Patrick included in his *Confession* the words of an early Creed, which he knew by heart. In his writing about his beliefs, he mentions the gift of God's grace repeatedly. He relied upon this active love of God to carry him through many difficulties. He never grew tired of emphasising that through God's love, and not through any special skill of his own, he had been able to accomplish great things in the face of enemies who despised Christianity and those who misunderstood the faith and tried too often to live independently without a proper understanding of God's grace. Patrick, at his best, put God first – whatever the problem might be.

LOOKING AHEAD TO THE END

Patrick had the distinct feeling that the end of the world was very near. The sacking of the City of Rome and the fall of the Empire seemed in those days to mark the end of civilisation. Patrick's journey as a bishop to bring the Gospel to thousands who had not heard of Christ must have seemed like the end of a long expedition which had brought him to the farthest outward edge of Europe.

HIS WORDS HAVE WEIGHT

There was more than enough work waiting for Patrick in the island of his adoption. He did it all for love. He admits that although he was born and brought up in Britain, he became Irish. He felt Irish. His writing in Latin has been criticised as rather stiff and formal. When we recall that he had a choice of three languages for his teaching and preaching, it is not surprising that he apologises for the stiffness of his Latin style. For conversation, he probably spoke in Celtic-British as a child and in Ireland it is likely that he used Celtic-Irish to talk to the people whom he loved to meet in their own houses. Both these languages were spoken rather than written.

WORDS OF LOVE AND POWER

Patrick spoke about his ministry in images. He had a lovely phrase for his pastoral work, preaching and visiting.

He called it 'hunting and fishing'. He borrowed the phrase from the Hebrew prophets of the Bible and found that it suited the Irish countryside, through which he wandered as a pilgrim for Christ. He hunted after people. He was concerned for their souls and bodies. He fished patiently for them, looking out for a good catch. In this spirit of simple confidence, he came into direct, personal touch with people, young and old. He bravely went out to meet them. He tried to persuade them to improve their lives and find a better way.

Before Patrick came to their homes and their families and tribes, many were held in the grip of strange fears and superstitions. They were terrified of the dark side of life. The true faith proclaimed by Patrick banished many fears and brought a new freedom to those who were baptised and confirmed in the life and membership of the Church.

Patrick speaks of God as Father, Son and Holy Spirit when he refers to his beliefs in his *Confession*. This word-picture of God as three persons in one was used by him to explain to his followers that God's love was shown first when he created the world, second when Jesus Christ came into the world, and third, through the Holy Spirit whose love and power works among all the peoples of the world. Many years after Patrick's time the Christians in Ireland sang a hymn about the Trinity, the three-personed God. The words of this 'Breastplate' hymn summed up the important things about God's love and protection. The followers of Patrick pictured him singing:

I bind unto myself today
The strong name of the Trinity
By invocation of the same
The three-in-one and one-in-three.

FROM DARKNESS INTO LIGHT

The song made clear to the faithful Christians that they need not fear the dark nor any of the frightening superstitions which prevented many people from enjoying life and sharing the freedom which the God of love gave to them.

The 'Breastplate' described how the Christians knew that they were protected by God:

Against the demon snares of sin,
Against all Satan's spells and wiles,
Against the wizard's evil craft,
Against the death-wound and the burning,
The choking wave, the poisoned shaft.

The druids were important people in Ireland at a time when there were many kings ruling over quite small kingdoms. They advised the kings when problems of State and government needed attention and were also in charge of the education of the young. They had a deep knowledge of poetry and laws and altogether seemed to be people of great influence. We have no writings to inform us about what they taught or prophesied. All their activities were carried out by word of mouth. There was, of course, a good side to their work. Not all druids were forceful and domineering. Some of their laws and their counselling as well as their teaching and healing work did much good.

Patrick, however, was guided by God to challenge the beliefs of the druids and reading between the lines of his *Confession* it seems that the only power he used as he moved among the people was the power of love. He won the confidence of the kings who listened to his preaching. They were attracted by his friendly personality. They saw how he cared for individuals and that he was anxious to show them a better way of life. There had not been much charity or love in paganism.

Kings entrusted their children to Patrick who educated them and trained them to help him in his task of spreading the Gospel. These pupils went with him on his pilgrimages, as 'he wandered about the country for Christ'. When Patrick's message was heard and taken to heart, it brought something new and hopeful to people's lives and dispelled their fears of the unknown and the mysterious.

HIGHEST STANDARDS

In the *Confession*, Patrick tells us about one particular Irishwoman, an aristocrat from one of the royal families, and very beautiful. When she heard about Jesus Christ, she wanted to give her life to follow and serve him. Patrick urged her to remain unmarried so that she might devote herself entirely to the service of God. Her family was very troubled about this and objected to the suggestion that she should not marry. They persecuted her and attacked Patrick, too. There was a real family row. All that happened makes us realise that in those days it was not at all easy to become a Christian, with freedom to choose between the single or the married life.

Slaves, as well as those who belonged to important ruling families, had difficult experiences to face when they became Christian and received baptism. Suddenly their eyes were opened to see how free the life of a Christian could be – so different from the laws that bound the slaves. The problem was that those slaves who became Christians still remained slaves. They were not very popular with their masters on account of their new outlook on life. In spite of threats and fearful suffering, the slaves bravely spoke out for the truth. They showed that each individual was counted as important in the eyes of God.

THOUSANDS FLOCK TO PATRICK

Patrick discovered how close his friendship was with those who suffered so much for their faith. He confirmed many of those he had baptised with prayer as he laid hands on their heads with a blessing. Some of these, later on, he ordained to minister in the Church. Against all expectations, Patrick's mission to Ireland became most successful. If sometimes he thought of moving elsewhere to work as a bishop, perhaps to Gaul, or Britain, he soon found himself declaring that he could not take such a step. When he said that he felt himself 'bound' in the 'Spirit', he meant that he had decided to spend the rest of his life in Ireland among the Christian converts whom he loved so dearly. He knew that it would be sinful to leave them. He did not claim to be perfect or free from faults and mistakes. He found out that there were many other Christians in his

*Baptising in the name of the Father and of the Son
and of the Holy Spirit.*

flock who were far better than he was. He thanked God for 'the life of perfection' they were leading. Patrick was so humble that he could not be jealous of others.

FACING HIS CRITICS AND HIS ENEMIES

Many of those whom Patrick met on his journeys through Ireland jeered at him. Although they laughed at him and scoffed on these occasions, he never gave in. He always spoke out bravely about his faith and refused to be silenced. He spoke about his own happiness and told others about the signs of God's goodness that he had been shown throughout his own life. He told people not only of the wonders of God's help in dangerous moments but also how patient God was with his 'silliness'. He praised God for having pity on him on the many thousands of occasions when he had been careless and foolish.

Patrick could not help thinking of all the grumblers at home in Britain who had warned him of the risks and dangers he would face in Ireland.

Patrick kept his faith firmly in spite of many temptations and trials, although very often he had to be careful. For example, he knew it would be wrong to receive gifts when he was welcoming new members into the Church. Jewels were sometimes showered upon him by grateful friends. Valuable and precious as these presents were, he knew that he must not appear to receive rewards, or even bribes, for any spiritual blessings that came to them through Patrick. He gave everything back to these generous donors. He wrote, in his quaint style, 'Perhaps when I baptised so many thousands of people I expected even half a farthing from one of them. Tell me if I did receive this tiniest coin – which would not even buy a shoe, and I will give it back.'

VOLUNTARY SERVICE

He certainly did not make any profit out of his preaching. Indeed he had many expenses as he journeyed. Patrick was known as 'a travelling man', and tramped on foot through many danger spots, far off any beaten track to parts of the island rarely visited. He knew that he was not the very first person to bring Christianity to Ireland, but he was certainly a pioneer, continually breaking new ground. Many places were untouched by the Christian faith before Patrick's missionary journeys.

We find him giving presents to kings. He paid salaries to those of their sons who travelled around with him, helping him in his ministry. In spite of all this, he was arrested on one alarming occasion and nearly killed. He was robbed and chained up in irons, but happily after fourteen days he was set free. Some close friends – and the Lord – he wrote, rescued him from this disaster.

Patrick mentioned some lawyers whom he met on his travels. They acted as advisers to the kings who had to make decisions and pass judgements when wrongdoers were brought before them. Patrick, as a Church leader, did not go to Law when he was attacked and threatened. His happy temperament and his readiness to forgive had enormous influence even among those who were ready to capture or kill him. He felt no fear and never seemed to lose his nerve. His good example showed up the greed

In danger often – Patrick was arrested, robbed and imprisoned,
but soon rescued again by his friends.

and selfishness of those who were his enemies. They couldn't understand why Patrick worked so strenuously for the love of people and not for any money or material possessions.

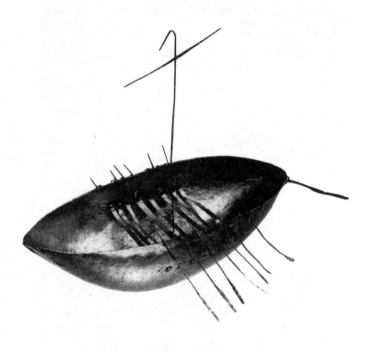

A gold model of a Celtic boat uncovered at Broighter, Co. Derry. It may have been an offering to a sea god, and dates from the first century BC.

CHAPTER X

The Angry Letter

Patrick certainly loved people, and sometimes he had to stand up for them when they were treated unjustly. In the well-known *Letter*, which he wrote to Coroticus, a chieftain-king in southern Scotland who had taken some of Patrick's newly confirmed Christians as captives, we learn how stern and strong Ireland's saint could be when there were innocent people to be rescued and defended.

Patrick became deeply angry when Coroticus, who claimed to be a Christian, treated these Christians whom he had enslaved very badly. Patrick knew it was his duty to speak the uncomfortable truth in love and in indignation because a great injustice had been done. In his *Letter* he protested to Coroticus and his soldiers, and quotes many words from the scriptures to support his complaints.

The *Letter* was an open one. Patrick wanted it to be read out in public. It was actually addressed to the soldiers who had been responsible for such fierce cruelty, but Patrick asked them to read it in the presence of Coroticus, their commanding officer. The commander had to be made aware of his responsibility for what had happened. Innocent people had been wrongly attacked.

An earlier letter, which has been lost, had been sent privately to the soldiers in the hope that some agreement could be found so that the victims of the attack could be sent back to Ireland speedily and peacefully. That letter, however, had been received with jeers and loud, mocking laughter. Patrick described this with the Latin word *cachinnos*, which has a scoffing sound. We can hear the sarcastic 'cackle' of the soldiers when we read the word out loud. Patrick had tried to buy back the captives and that offer was treated as a bad joke.

A letter of any kind was something very special in those days, when there was no such thing as a regular delivery of mail. This particular *Letter* from a bishop, written for all to hear, expressed the hope that Coroticus would be ashamed of what he had done and would be ready to change his mind. Patrick saw himself as an ambassador for Christ. He said that he had a perfect right to send this message even if this 'tyrant' Coroticus was in Scotland and not in Ireland. Patrick was representing his King, the God who was made known in Christ. If Patrick preached the love of God, he also had to uphold the justice of God. A great injustice had clearly been done to people who were in no position to defend themselves.

It is a moving letter. It is addressed sometimes to the soldiers and sometimes to Coroticus himself. Patrick writes in a loving way about his dear Christians now suffering as slaves. Some of them had already been sold for a great price to unknown owners. Patrick thinks of their white Confirmation robes and the sweet smell of the ointment used on their foreheads when they were anointed at Confirmation.

He writes in the *Letter*, 'What am I to do, Lord?' He hopes God will hear this cry for help when it is read out too: 'Lord, I am thoroughly despised. See, your sheep are torn to pieces around me and are carried off by the raiders, as ordered by the evil-hearted Coroticus.'

Patrick certainly did not mince his words. He knew how greedy these raiders had been. As we read the *Letter* we can feel how very angry he was. His short sentences are sharp and pointed. He writes passionately since he had known at first-hand what it was like to be captured and carried away to a strange country.

He hopes that his words to Coroticus and the soldiers will bring some comfort to those who have been so greatly wronged. Patrick was very stern when he announced to the public and to anyone who might have contact with these guilty people: 'You must not associate with them, or seek any favours from any of them. It is not right to eat or drink with them. No one ought to receive any gifts or alms from them. Such fraternising must not take place until they make amends to God and pay painful penalties, until they set free these servants of God and these baptised handmaids of Christ for whom he was crucified.' This was the meaning of Patrick's words of excommunication.

PART II

CHAPTER 9

Later Times – the Stories, Legends and Great Traditions

The *Confession* and the *Letter* have introduced us to Patrick. Many stories are told by others about him. He has been remembered through the centuries for his preaching and teaching of Christianity.

He was a bishop, guiding and protecting his flock, before mitres were worn or croziers were held by bishops in Ireland. (Mitres were not worn in Ireland until five hundred years after Patrick's time, and the crozier he carried was probably a simple wooden staff.) When storytellers told tales of Patrick banishing snakes from Ireland, they probably meant that he drove out what was evil and brought in what was good. Much, much later still, in the eighteenth century, the picture of the shamrock with its three leaves springing from one stem came into tales and

*Bronze hilt of a short, triangular, iron sword, with
decorative knob and triangular breastpiece. It shows the
Roman influence and dates from the first century BC.
It was caught in a fishing net in Ballyshannon Bay, Co. Donegal.*

lessons about Patrick's teaching that God was Tri-une, that is, a three-personed God with life and love expressed by Father, Son and Spirit bound together and united in a close relationship.

The word 'shamrock' (*seamróg* in Irish), which is now associated with the lesser yellow trefoil *(trifolium minus)*, seems to be derived from the word for 'rivet' in the Irish language – *seam* (pronounced sham). Some scholars think that the three rivets on the hilt of the first-century sword *(opposite)* may symbolise the 'three-in-one' God.

Patrick has also been honoured in songs, ballads and hymns through the centuries. The Book of Armagh, one of the treasures in the Library of Trinity College, Dublin, notes that Patrick died on 17 March. That book, written four hundred years after Patrick's time, refers to the custom which arose in honour of the national saint 'always to chant his Gaelic canticle' on his festival day. The tradition ran that he sang, 'Christ be with me' (*Críost liom*) and prayed the words of what later became known as the 'Breastplate' hymn.

CHAPTER 10

The Book of Armagh

The atmosphere of ancient, historic Armagh still surrounds the ninth-century manuscript. We find in its pages repeated references to the city's name. It is quaintly spelt, sometimes as *Ardd-Machae*, or again as *Altum Mache*.

The book was written in a monastery where prayer, study and all sorts of domestic work filled the programme of each day. In the book, we read of the Irish Church both at worship and out among the people, teaching and preaching. Mention is made of the hymns they sang and the words they spoke: the sacraments of Baptism and Eucharist are linked with the study and life of the monastic community.

In the workshop their craftsmanship in bronze and wood became famous. Assicus, the smith, worked in bronze and silver to furnish the sanctuary on the Hill of

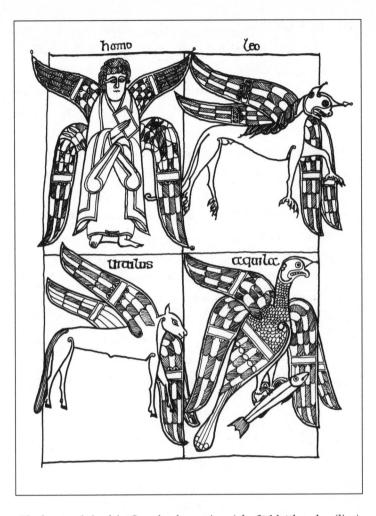

The four symbols of the Gospels – homo *(man) for St Matthew,* leo *(lion) for St Mark,* vitulus *(calf) for St Luke and* aquila *(eagle) for St John. These drawings illustrate the beautifully decorated Book of Armagh.*

Armagh with sacred vessels. In the writing-place (*scripto-rium*) the scribes were highly honoured for the skill of copying and decorating the manuscripts, such as the Book of Armagh. This book is now in the Library of Trinity College, Dublin, together with other Irish manuscripts, such as the Book of Durrow and the Book of Kells. The Book of Armagh was known as Patrick's 'testament'. It contains the earliest piece of writing in Irish history – Patrick's *Confession* – a *Life of Patrick* by Muirchú and another book of *Memoirs* and *Sayings (Dicta* in Latin) about Patrick by Tirechán.

Also within the covers of this book, which is now bound in two volumes, is the Book of the Angel, which tells of the importance of Armagh as a Christian centre. A *Life of St Martin of Tours* was included to provide some account of the background of Patrick's training for his ministry. There is a strong tradition, although this story is often mingled with legend, that Patrick had his clerical training in a French (Gaulish) monastery. Famous, too, in this book is the earliest known Latin New Testament to be found in Ireland.

We are fortunate to have Muirchú's *Life*, which has many quotations from Patrick's *Confession*. Yet we know that since Muirchú wrote so long after Patrick's death, legends are quite clearly mixed in with history; stories about Patrick have been passed from mouth to mouth and have been exaggerated in the telling. This often happens when no written evidence has survived. We cannot be certain that popular accounts of one who was so greatly admired in Ireland, as Patrick obviously was, are completely accurate and free from bias.

CHAPTER 11

Muirchú

About two hundred years after Patrick's death, Muirchú wrote a *Life* of Ireland's leading saint. He was encouraged to do so by one of the bishops, named Áed, from Sletty (Co. Laois), in the midlands. He realised the difficulty of his task and describes himself as a rather nervous author who has heard much about Patrick, but cannot always be sure of his facts. It was hard for him to know the difference between the legends and the history that surrounded Patrick.

Yet often the seeds of truth and hard fact lie hidden in fantastic legends. In the days before records and reminiscences were written down, a very small incident could soon become exaggerated. We know what is meant by a 'fishing story' among anglers who speak with pride of the size of their lost catch. So it came about that a sign of Patrick's great faith could easily become a miracle with some magical additions. A miracle can happen, but sometimes it is tempting to emphasise the wonder-work in the very terms that soothsayers and wizards were fond of using in the days of the druids.

Muirchú received encouragement from one Cogitosus, whom he called his 'father'. Cogitosus may have really been Muirchú's patron and instructor; he had written a *Life of Saint Brigit* of Kildare. Muirchú with his *Life of Patrick* would point to the leadership of Armagh, the city which even today is called the ecclesiastical capital of Ireland.

A HUMBLE WRITER

Muirchú in his introduction, addressing 'My Lord Áed', the bishop, writes in the style of Luke, the evangelist, in the opening words of his Gospel. Both writers attempt to tell the correct version of their story, drawn from the many different versions that exist. Muirchú is so conscious of the difficulty he faces in making a connected story out of the rumours and whispers about Patrick that he feels he must tell the world about his problem. He writes:

'I have taken my little talent, like the boys who make their first speech in the schoolplay. I take a boy's paddle-boat, as it were, out on the deep and dangerous sea of my holy story. The waves rise to towering heights among the sharp rocks hidden in the waters. No boat apart from my father Cogitosus's has ventured forth on such a sea.'

Muirchú goes on:

'I do not want to give the impression that I want to make something big out of something small. I shall try to describe, bit by bit, and step by step, a few of the numerous deeds of Patrick, with my little knowledge of my sources, from an unreliable memory, written in a poor style, but prompted by my great affection for holy Patrick ...'

The Book of Armagh, in which Muirchú's *Life of Patrick* appears, also has a copy of the *Life of St Martin*, written by Sulpicius Severus. This may have been a model biography to help Muirchú with his writing. The seventh century also saw Adomnán's *Life of Columba*. In this period of monastic life, the Church's history was taught through the lives and experiences of outstanding Christian leaders – Brigit, Columba, Martin, Adomnán and, of course, Patrick.

Muirchú fills out the story which Patrick told about himself in the *Confession*. Even if he admits that he cannot be certain of his facts, he counts it important to pass on to others what traditions and rumours were going around among the Christians who felt they owed much to Patrick's leadership.

From Muirchú's *Life* we learn that Patrick went to France after he escaped from his life as a slave in Ireland. When he found Germanus (AD380–448), who was in charge of Auxerre and clearly a very important Church leader in France, Patrick stayed with him and received training for his future missionary work in the monastery. Germanus was an inspiration. Patrick sat at his feet 'just as Paul sat at the feet of Gamaliel'. While there, news came of the death of Palladius who had been sent to look after the

Christians in Ireland. Palladius had scarcely been there a year when his appointment came to an abrupt end.

At this point in the story, Patrick was made a bishop by Amator. Together with two companions, Auxilius and Iserninus, he set sail across the sea to Ireland once more.

PATRICK MEETS THE HEATHEN KING

Soon we hear of Patrick's encounter with Loegaire 'the fierce heathen emperor of the barbarians who reigned in Tara'. This king had been told by the 'wizards, soothsayers and enchanters' who surrounded the royal court at Tara in the plain of Co. Meath that there was trouble ahead. Loegaire was greatly disturbed by these gazers into the future. He heard that 'a certain foreign practice like a kingdom' would be introduced from across the sea to kill the kings in Ireland; the people would be won over by this strange teaching, and all the local gods would be destroyed.

This prophecy was puzzling and the words of magic were frightening. They sounded like poetry when recited as follows:

Adze-head shall come,
With his crooked-headed staff
And his house with a hole in its head.
He shall chant blasphemy from his table,
From the eastern part of his house,
And all his household will answer him:
'So be it, so be it.'
When all this happens
Our kingdom, which is heathen, shall not stand.

Things of the strangest kind certainly did begin to happen. It was the year when there was a very special festival at Tara. The idols were worshipped with magical ceremonies. All sorts of enchantments and idolatries were performed in the presence of kings, governors, commanders and other very important persons. Muirchú compared the scene with Babylon in the time of King Nebuchadnezzar.

PATRICK CELEBRATES EASTER

All this happened on the very night when Patrick was celebrating the Christian Easter festival not far away across the plains of Meath. Patrick lit a holy fire. Its bright blaze gleamed in the darkness and was seen for miles across the plain as far as Tara.

'In the beginning'
(in principio) – *the first words of St John's Gospel, taken from the Book of Armagh.*

The king cried: 'What is this? Who is it who has dared to commit this sacrilege in my kingdom? Let him be put to death.'

The elders and councillors replied to the king: 'O king, live for ever. This fire which we see and was lit this night before one was lit in your house, that is, in the palace of Tara, will never be put out, never, unless it is put out this night on which it has been lit.'

King Loegaire was greatly alarmed to hear this. He felt like King Herod. He went out intending to kill and destroy. He took with him twenty-two chariots and two of his best qualified wizards and made for Slane, where Patrick was.

The wizards advised the king not to go too near to the fire Patrick had lit. Patrick was then summoned by the king to come forward. He came, with the brave words of a psalm on his lips:

Some may go in chariots,
And some on horses,
But we will walk in the name of our God.

One of the king's company was convinced that Patrick had the true faith. He was the only one to rise to his feet. His name was Erc. Patrick blessed him. The others began to insult Patrick and to curse the Christian faith. Patrick answered with a prayer, asking God to deal with these enemies. A wizard met his death; he fell to the ground, and his skull struck a stone.

Chaos followed. The king threatened while Patrick prayed: 'Let God arise and let his enemies be scattered. Let those that hate Him flee before Him.'

Darkness fell. An earthquake overthrew the chariots. Everyone retreated in confusion.

Then the queen spoke to Patrick. She asked him not to destroy the king. She said that the king would come and worship Patrick's Lord. The king came, but he only pretended to worship the Christian god. He still wanted to kill Patrick and tried to trick the saint and his companions. The story continues, with an astonishing surprise:

'The king counted [Patrick and his followers] as they approached and immediately they disappeared clean out of the king's sight. The heathen saw just eight deer with a fawn, heading for the wilds.'

The next day was a time for feasting in the palace at Tara. It was Easter Day and Patrick with his companions came to preach and to declare, "Jesus Christ is risen today." Only one person stood up. This time it was Dubtach.

The heathen king cunningly invited Patrick to come and eat at his feast. Patrick accepted the invitation. Drink was poured into his cup. A wizard added a drop to it. Patrick blessed the cup and the liquid froze like ice.

When the cup was turned upside down only the drop which the wizard had poured in fell out. Patrick blessed the cup a second time and the liquid returned to its natural state, amazing everyone.'

'The cup was turned upside down; the deadly drop fell out.'

THE HEATHEN KING BECOMES CHRISTIAN

The wizards tried all sorts of magic, but each time they failed to impress Patrick. Patrick's prayers seemed to spoil all their efforts. The king was in despair. 'It is better for me to believe than to die,' he said.

The king believed that day. Patrick said that although the king's days at Tara would be prolonged, no member of his royal family would be king after him because Loegaire had attacked Patrick's teaching and had stood in his way, opposing his message.

PATRICK SEEKS HIS OLD MASTER

Patrick's name is associated with many places in the north of Ireland. Muirchú tells us of people and districts with names which Patrick never mentioned in his *Confession*. For example, the master who owned Patrick as a young slave boy is given the name Miliucc.

When Patrick, by this time a bishop, lands at the harbour of Inverdee 'laden with wonderful sacred treasures from across the sea', he is determined to set out to pay Miliucc a double ransom for release from his bonds of slavery. We hear of him in Co. Down at Strangford Lough. One named Dichu, 'a pagan but good at heart', makes friends with him. Very soon, at a place called Sabhall or Saul, near Downpatrick, where it is said that Patrick died, this Dichu becomes a Christian. Patrick pressed on to Mount Slemish, in what is now Co. Antrim, near Ballymena, to find Miliucc. This part of Ireland was called the country of the Cruithne.

Muirchú writes: 'It was from this mountain that long before, when he had been in slavery as a captive there, Patrick saw the angel Victoricus before his very eyes ascend swift-footed into heaven and leave the imprint of his step on the rock of the other mountain.'

Miliucc was alarmed at the thought of his former slave, Patrick, coming to visit him. 'To avoid being subjected to his slave lording it over him,' he made a great fire, setting alight all his possessions, and throwing himself into the flames, preferring to be burned to death rather than to be humiliated.'

When Patrick discovered what had happened there on the south side of Mount Slemish, he exclaimed: 'I do not know, but God knows; this man, this king who consigned himself to the flames to avoid believing at the end of his life and serving the eternal God … I do not know, but God knows … his descendants shall be slaves for ever.'

A SITE FOR HIS CHURCH

Soon Armagh comes into Muirchú's story. Patrick wanted a place for Christian worship. He asked Daire, a rich and respected citizen, to give him a site for a church.

The wealthy man said to the saint: 'What place do you want?'

'I want you to give me that piece of high ground, which is called Willow Ridge [Drumsill] and I shall build a place there.'

But Daire refused to give the saint the high ground, and gave him instead another site on lower ground, which is now the Martyrs' Graveyard near Armagh, and Patrick

lived there with his followers.

There soon followed a row between Daire and Patrick. A dispute had occurred over a horse who came in to graze on the ground given to Patrick. The horse died and the groom blamed Patrick for killing the animal. Daire determined to kill the Christian, but, as he spoke, he himself suddenly dropped dead. Patrick went to him and, with prayer and sprinkled water, brought both Daire and the horse back to life.

Daire's attitude towards Patrick changed after this and he wanted to present him with a very special gift, 'a wonderful bronze bowl'. Also, he climbed up with Patrick to the high ground, the Hill of Armagh, where they found a hind with her little fawn lying on the spot where there is now the altar of the North Church in Armagh. Patrick's companions wanted to kill the fawn, but Patrick did not allow this. He carried it gently on his shoulders and, with the hind following, let the fawn go free in another wood on the north side of Armagh.

'Since many have tried to tell the story ...'
The opening of St Luke's Gospel in the Book of Armagh.

MIRACLES AND WONDER-WORKING

Muirchú writes of Patrick's miracles and wonder-works. At the end of his biography he also makes mention, very briefly, of Coroticus, that 'very great persecutor and murderer of Christians', the subject of the *Letter* written by Patrick.

We see in many of the incidents which were collected and described in Muirchú's life, the outstanding qualities of Patrick's life which are also apparent in the *Confession* and the *Letter*. His faith, so firm that it overpowered many who were fearful and jealous of this Christian visitor, shines through the meetings and encounters. He has no need to kill his enemies. Through prayer he confronts them with God's power and judgement. Small wonder that his spiritual weapons, described in the famous 'Breastplate of St Patrick', still bring protection and strength to the followers of the faith that the saint established in a troubled and dangerous country. These traditional words are still sung today:

I bind unto myself today
The power of God to hold and lead
His eye to watch, his might to stay
His ear to hearken to my need.
The wisdom of my God to teach
His hand to guide, his shield to ward;
The word of God to give me speed,
His heavenly host to be my guard.

CHAPTER 12

Tirechán

Tirechán's writings in the Book of Armagh are more like memoirs and statistics. He does not write a systematic account of Patrick's life in the orderly style of Muirchú. For that reason he is less interesting.

However, he was clearly fascinated by the names of persons and places. He gives a long list of the successors of Patrick and is anxious to link them with the importance of Armagh as a Christian centre and the leading church in the country.

There is also another side to the account of Patrick's travels which he gives us in great detail. Tirechán was a bishop in Connaught. Consequently, he pays special attention to Patrick's journeys. Three times, he tells us, Patrick crossed the Shannon. At the Ford of the Two Birds, he makes his way through Roscommon, Mayo, Sligo and Leitrim. The Moy river, and many another stream, feature

The king's daughters ask Patrick,
'Where have you come from?'

in the fishing stories of the saint. Patrick blessed one river (the Drowes) and it gains a good name for the many large fish that swim in it. On the other hand, he does anything but bless another stream, the Duff, which divides Leitrim from Sligo, because the fishing family that lived on its banks refused to share any of their catch with him as he passed by. The fishing was declared to be very bad there after that piece of inhospitality! Another river, the Séle, suffered condemnation from Patrick because two of the saint's disciples drowned in it.

MAIDENS AT THE WELL

Among all the names of people and places in Patrick's elaborate and often apparently circular journey through the west of Ireland, a lovely story is included.

Patrick meets the daughters of King Loegaire at the well of Clébach. These two girls, fair-haired Ethne and red-headed Fedelma, have come to wash in the waters of the well. They are surprised to find Patrick and a whole gathering of bishops there – a kind of synod!

The maidens thought that it was a dream and that they were seeing something that felt like fantasy, springing out of their vivid imaginations. Yet they had courage enough to start a conversation with this great gathering. They asked, 'Where have you come from?'

Patrick replied: 'It would be better if you stated your belief rather than asked us questions.'

Ethne then said, 'Who is God? Where is he? Whose God is he? Where does he live? Has your God sons and daughters, gold and silver? Is he alive and beautiful? Have many fostered his son, are his daughters dear and beautiful? Is he in the sky or earth, or in the water, in rivers, or mountains, or valleys? How can he be seen and loved? Is he in youth or old age?'

Patrick replied: 'Our God is the God of all, Heaven and Earth, sea and rivers, of the sun, moon and all the stars, high mountains and low valleys, above heaven, in heaven, under heaven. He breathes in all things, makes all things live, supports all things ... He lights the sun, makes wells ...

'He has a Son, co-eternal with Him, the Son is not younger than the Father nor is the Father older than the Son, and the Holy Spirit breathes in them. The Father and the Son and the Holy Spirit are not separate.

'I wish to join you to the heavenly King since you are daughters of an earthly king.'

The two girls then asked how this could be done. In answer to further questions from Patrick, they declared that they believed. They were baptised with a white garment over their heads. They received the Eucharist ... and then they died. Two of the druids who were present became Christians after this.

MOSES AND PATRICK

Tirechán was very fond of numbers in his story of Patrick. He compares the Irish saint with Moses, the great leader of the Israelites. Moses led the Jewish people out of their slavery in Egypt through a wilderness to a fruitful and sunny promised land. In his notes about Patrick, Tirechán tells us that the saint was like Moses in four ways:

'Wandering about for Christ' –
a pilgrimage up Croagh Patrick.

1. He heard an angel speaking out of a thornbush.
2. He fasted forty days and forty nights.
3. He spent one-hundred-and-twenty years in this present life.
4. Nobody knows where his bones were laid to rest.

Tirechán calculated the age of Patrick in this way: aged seven, he was baptised; ten years later, he was captured; for seven years he was a slave; for thirty years he studied for the ministry; for seventy-two years he taught the faith; his entire age was one-hundred-and-twenty, just like Moses!

Many of the stories recounted by Tirechán remind us of the legends told about Patrick's influence. Druids drop dead when Patrick raises his hand to God. When Patrick loses a tooth, it is treasured by one of his companions.

Croagh Patrick made him think of the mountain-top experiences of Moses and Elijah and Christ. Ireland had its own Mount Sinai, Mount Carmel and the Mount of Transfiguration.

Tirechán describes the vision: 'Patrick proceeded to the summit of the mountain, climbing Cruachán Aigli, and stayed there forty days and forty nights, and birds annoyed him and he could not see the face of sky and land and sea, the past – the present and the future – God said to him: "Climb, O holy man, to the top of the mountain which towers above and is higher than all the mountains to the west of the sun, in order to bless the people of Ireland."'

Tirechán pays less attention to the early part of Patrick's

life. Places, family names, personalities and churches are his chief interest. We travel with him, as he traces Patrick the traveller, first in Co. Meath where Bishop Ultan, Tirechán's patron, lived at Ardbraccan, near Navan. Then follows the journey across the Shannon, through Connaught, in Tirechán's own home country in the west of Ireland.

CHAPTER 13

The Book of the Angel

Another document from the Book of Armagh, probably written before Muirchú's *Life of Patrick* and Tirechán's *Memoirs*, is the Book of the Angel. It opens with a conversation between an angel and Patrick. The scene is a well close to the city of Armagh. Patrick has been baptising, teaching and healing crowds who have come to him.

While he was waiting for more to come 'from everywhere for the knowledge of the faith', Patrick fell asleep.

An angel woke him with a gentle touch. 'Have I done anything wrong?' the startled Patrick asked.

'No,' said the angel, who appreciated all the hard work Patrick had undertaken. 'The Lord your God,' the angel went on, 'knows that your present place which we see before us, placed high on the hill, is narrow and has only a small church, and is also hemmed in by some inhabitants in the neighbourhood and the surrounding territory is not sufficient to give shelter to all.

'Therefore, a vast piece of church land [*terminus*] is being established by the Lord for the city of Armagh, which you have loved more than all the lands of the Irish ... and, further, the Lord God has given all the tribes of the Irish as a *paruchia* [a kind of diocese] to you and to this city, which in Irish is named *Ardd-Machae*.'

The writer of the Book of the Angel continues: 'Let us now speak of the special reverence for Armagh and of the honour for the bishop of this same city.

'Now this city has been established by God as supreme and free and has been specially dedicated by the angel of God and by the apostolic man, the holy bishop Patrick. It, therefore, has precedence, by a certain privilege and by the heavenly authority of the supreme bishop, its founder, over all churches and monasteries of all the Irish.

LI – the first two letters of 'Liber' (the book) – at the beginning of St Matthew's Gospel, 'the book of the genealogy of Jesus Christ', in the Book of Armagh.

'Between holy Patrick and Brigit, pillars of the Irish Church, there existed so great a friendship of charity that they were of one heart and one mind ...

'Patrick said: "O my Brigit, your *paruchia* will be deemed to be in your province in your dominion, but in the eastern and western part it will be in my domination."'

PART III

CHAPTER 14

In Conclusion

The spirit of Patrick is very much alive today. He is a worldwide figure, a saint of international stature.

Wherever the Irish are to be found in the five continents, there will always be a group in each city and country town to celebrate the memory of the nation's saint on 17 March each year – the month and the day mentioned in the pages of the Book of Armagh.

A FESTIVAL DAY

On that day, the festivities are marked by worship and song. It is also a notable day for strengthening the spirit of fellowship among those whose roots spring from the four provinces of the island. There is a deep unity in such a celebration: north and south, east and west put their complicated history in the background to express their Irishness together at the festival.

It is a day of peacemaking and mutual understanding, abroad as well as at home. Many who are not Irish are eager to disclose a relationship, even of the most slender kind, hidden away in past generations. Such friendly harmony can be seen and heard when the bands play and the colourful processions are on the march through the principal streets of great cities far from the land of Patrick's adoption.

PAST MEETS PRESENT

New York City in America and Sydney in Australia, in their different ways, lift their banners and do honour to Patrick. In this century, such demonstrations of affection for the homeland, its culture and its traditions, both Celtic and Christian, have become more fully organised. There is history in such pageantry. Trade and industry also find a place in the parades.

WEARING THE GREEN

Many more than the Irish wear the green shamrock. This plant did not receive prominence until long after Patrick's life. It may be a disappointment for many to discover that its first mention occurs in the year 1727!

WORLDWIDE

Cathedrals and churches are to be found the world over with dedications and memorials in honour of St Patrick. A courageous missionary himself, his example continues to inspire the sons and daughters of Ireland to go into the world with the good news of the Gospel of Christ.

PROCESSIONS AND PILGRIMAGES

Not only processions commemorate him. Pilgrimages are another kind of spiritual adventure which Patrick's travels have inspired. The climbing of the 'Reek' is a strenuous journey for those who not only reach the summit of Croagh Patrick in Co. Mayo but accept the discipline of prayer and fasting on the steep, stony track which the pilgrims tread. There is poignancy felt there on the last Sunday in July before the August day (*Lughnasa*) – this day marks the emergence of Christianity from pre-Christian Celtic days.

Donegal's Lough Derg challenges those who endure the hardship with a characteristic Patrician spirit. Such a 'wandering about for Christ' has long been part of the religious heritage. In our day, happily, Christians of many varied traditions, even when not fully united in doctrine and liturgical life, are able to share visits to the sacred, ancient sites and to tread where Patrick may have trod, as twenty-first-century pilgrims. In Co. Down, at Saul and Downpatrick, as well as at Tara, the Christians, still separated, rejoice in the unity and welcoming fellowship which Patrick displayed.

IRELAND, HIS HOME

St Patrick himself should have the last word. His life was rough and rugged. He had to face jealousy and much cruel abuse. Yet he was brave to the end. A rare serenity shines through the inimitable style of his words:

*The ox, symbol of St Luke, with the other Gospel symbols
in its wings: man, lion and eagle.*

'Let anyone laugh and revile me who wants to,' he wrote, 'I will not keep silence nor will I conceal the signs and wonders which have been shown me by the Lord.'

*The Eagle – symbol of St John – with the fish, the symbol of Jesus,
in its claws. In its feathered wings the symbols of St Matthew (man),
St Mark (lion) and St Luke (ox) can be seen.*